T0080824

BIRDS OF PREY

Peregrine FALCONS

by Melissa Hill

Consulting Editor: Gail Saunders-Smith, PhD

Consultant: Jessica Ehrgott, Bird and Mammal
Trainer, Downtown Aquarium, Denver

CAPSTONE PRESS
a capstone imprint

Pebble Plus is published by Capstone Press,
1710 Roe Crest Drive, North Mankato, Minnesota 56003
www.capstonepub.com

Library of Congress Cataloging-in-Publication Data
Hill, Melissa, 1975–
Peregrine falcons / by Melissa Hill.
pages cm.—(Pebble plus. Birds of Prey)
Includes bibliographical references and index.
Summary: "Describes the characteristics, habitat, behavior, life cycle, and
threats to peregrine falcons"—Provided by publisher.
Audience: Ages 5 to 8.
Audience: Grades K to 3.
ISBN 978-1-4914-2092-8 (library binding)
ISBN 978-1-4914-2310-3 (pbk.)
ISBN 978-1-4914-2333-2 (ebook pdf)
1. Peregrine falcon—Juvenile literature. I. Title.
QL696.F34H55 2014
598.9′6—dc23   2014032782

Editorial Credits
Jeni Wittrock, editor; Peggie Carley and Janet Kusmierski, designers;
Svetlana Zhurkin, media researcher; Katy LaVigne, production specialist

Photo Credits
Alamy: blickwinkel, 5; Minden Pictures: Konrad Wothe, 7, Martin Dohrn, 15;
Newscom: Photoshot/NHPA/Alan Williams, 17, Photoshot/NHPA/Dave Watts,
19; Shutterstock: balounm, back cover (background), Chris Hill, 1, 9, Michael
G. McKinne, cover, back cover, Steve Oehlenschlager, 11, StockPhotoAstur, 13,
taviphoto, 21

Note to Parents and Teachers

The Birds of Prey set supports national science standards related to
life science. This book describes and illustrates peregrine falcons.
The images support early readers in understanding the text. The
repetition of words and phrases helps early readers learn new
words. This book also introduces early readers to subject-specific
vocabulary words, which are defined in the Glossary section. Early
readers may need assistance to read some words and to use the
Table of Contents, Glossary, Read More, Internet Sites, Critical
Thinking Using the Common Core, and Index sections of the book.

Table of Contents

Feathered Predator

A hunting peregrine falcon flies high. It spots a smaller bird below. The peregrine dives fast and grabs its meal with its feet.

When diving, peregrines
are faster than any other
animal. They may dive up
to 200 miles (322 kilometers)
per hour. That is fast!

Up Close!

Smooth gray feathers cover a peregrine's back. The falcon's underside has spots and stripes. Its head and cheeks are dark.

Strong chests and wings help peregrines fly fast. Their pointed wings slice through the air.

Peregrines have long toes
and talons to catch and
hold prey. Sharp, curved beaks
are perfect for eating meat.
Peregrines' main prey is birds.

Living on the Edge

Peregrine falcons live all over the world. Peregrines are found in deserts, grasslands, and even in cities.

Peregrine Falcon Range

⬭ where peregrine falcons live

Falcon Families

Many birds build nests with sticks. Not peregrines! They choose a high, rocky place to lay their eggs.

Peregrine falcons lay two
to four eggs each year.
In a month the eggs hatch.
Peregrine chicks learn to fly
and hunt in two months.

Life isn't easy for a falcon.
They can be hurt or killed
by great horned owls and
people. Wild peregrines
can live 10 or more years.

Glossary

beak—the hard front part of the mouth of a bird

chick—a young bird

prey—an animal that is hunted by another animal for food

slice—to move or cut through something smoothly and easily

talon—a sharp, curved claw

underside—the part of a bird's body that usually faces the ground

Read More

Jessell, Tim. *Falcon.* New York: Random House Books, 2012.

Lunis, Natalie. *Peregrine Falcon: Dive, Dive, Dive!* New York: Bearport Pub., 2010.

Sill, Cathryn P. *About Raptors.* About Series. Atlanta: Peachtree Publishers, 2010.

Internet Sites

FactHound offers a safe, fun way to find Internet sites related to this book. All of the sites on FactHound have been researched by our staff.

Here's all you do:

Visit *www.facthound.com*

Type in this code: 9781491420928

Super-cool stuff! Check out projects, games and lots more at **www.capstonekids.com**

Critical Thinking Using the Common Core

What are the main dangers to peregrine falcons?
(Key Ideas and Details)

How might peregrine falcons escape from predators?
(Integration of Knowledge and Ideas)

Index

Word Count: 191
Grade: 1
Early-Intervention Level: 14